T0064207

Inner creative *Girl*

**A little motivation to
create your dream career
or make it a business plan**

CAROL RAMOS

Order this book online at www.trafford.com
or email orders@trafford.com

Most Trafford titles are also available at major online book retailers.

Printed in the United States of America.

ISBN: 978-1-4669-8923-8 (sc)
ISBN: 978-1-4669-8922-1 (hc)
ISBN: 978-1-4669-8921-4 (e)

Library of Congress Control Number: 2013907061

Trafford rev. 05/20/2013

 www.trafford.com

North America & international
toll-free: 1 888 232 4444 (USA & Canada)
phone: 250 383 6864 ♦ fax: 812 355 4082

Contents

Dedication

Thank you Lord for giving me the opportunity to write this book, you are my number one inspiration for being the greatest artist of all times. I dedicate this book to my children for being my greatest motivation to work hard, my wonderful husband for being there for me and help me with all my projects. My husband's mom and dad for being so carrying and support me in every way. Thanks

Acknowledgments

Thank you Trafford publishing for all the support and work to make this inspirational books a reality for publishing. Thank you to all the team members of Trafford publishing that work hard for the realization of this project. I need to give thanks to Joel Berou, my publishing consultant for motivating to start this book project. To my husband who has being a lot of support for me by creating my website and helping me with other aspects of my business project. To his parent because they make my work easier by helping me with other tasks that I need to get done. I want to thank my children because they are my inspiration to move forward. Also I want to thank God because I have seeing His helping hand throughout my life experiences. Thank you!

Introduction

An essential aspect of creativity is not being afraid to fail

Edwin Land

I've got them written all over:

Phrases.
Bible verses.
Motivational quotes.
Movie lines.
Song lyrics.

$\mathscr{I}$ mean, who doesn't need a dose of inspiration when other people's opinions are screaming loudly in your ears. Let me get this straight in your mind, those opinions does not have to become your reality. Trust me, is extremely difficult to get out of your "comfort zone" when all you do is listening to all the noises of negativity. It took me years to understand that there's a sparkle in each one of us that make us different and make us the wonderful person we are. We all have dreams, aspirations and a whole world of opportunities lying before us. It is up to us to start thinking out of the box and let that inner creative girl work her way out. It will make for sure your life more fun and excited.

Since a little girl my passion was to become an artist, the small town plaza in Camuy, Puerto Rico became the stage where my imagination took its course. I visualized myself connecting with my audience, singing to thousands of people and being a famous celebrity. But wait a minute! Me! A celebrity! Huh? What kind of future can a poor girl with a difficult childhood profile have! A girl that became an orphan at the age of ten! Seriously, that could be the thoughts of any person in my shoes. Thank God my gradma make her appearance and adopt me, even though she had a totally different idea for my professional career, attending church with her was a turning point to discover my inner creative girl. But before that U-turn to become a inner creative girl took place, my biggest dilemma was being asked in High School what were my plans for my road trip to college. Feelings of insecurity and nervousness made my stomach twirl like an orchestra. What if I say that all I want to be was a singer or an actress or a professional in the art field? Well, that's not exactly what my gradma envision for me or that's not exactly what others think as a real career. But for me the only thing I want it to do was developed my creative skills in the area I was passionate about, the arts.

Fortunately, the church became the platform to acquire successful Leadership skills, polish those hidden talents and developed others that I didn't even know existed! Or I was even capable of doing! Don't get me wrong, it took one step at a time and a bunch of mistakes along the way to find ways to connect my inner creative girl with a career path that could pay my bills! While working as a youth Director, an awoken desire to learn more, embarked me in a college adventure that taught me important lessons that definitely will share with you. It took some experimentation and some risk to get out of my comfort zone and try something new, believe me I felt uncomfortable, I mean who wouldn't? You are getting out of that little zone where you being comfortable most of your life, I know that for sure, but once you decide to take your first step out, and face your fears you can discover who you really can be. The secret is to face your fear of the unknown or the fear to fail. When feeling of fears or failure come to my mind that's when I looked around and see it written everywhere (my motivational quotes);

Defeat is not the worst of failures. Not to have tried is the true failure

George E. Woodberry

Don't be afraid to fail. Don't waste energy trying to cover up failure, learn from your failures and go on to the next challenge. It's ok to fail. If you're not failing, you're not growing.

—H. Stanley Judd-

You gain strength, courage, and confidence by every experience in which you really stop to look fear in the face. You must do something which you think you cannot do.

—Eleanor Roosevelt-

In this Book you will find inspiration, tips to discover who you are and where you want go in life, ideas for a creative and inspiring career that brings you real fulfillment. You will also read stories of successful girls that worked the way out to great achievement, including myself! It doesn't matter how old are you; you'll find advice whether you're a college student wondering what's your next step in life or a thirty something mom that wants to start a business. You know, it's never too late! As you read through the pages of this book, let your creativity flow and uncover the various options you can think of, to make a living out of your passion. Maybe you start in a retail store like me and work your way up to small business entrepreneurship, maybe you start in your own gaining experiences that will lead you to be your own boss or continue polishing the skills that will take you to own that Job with the Company you always dream of. Whatever it is that you are dreaming to do, you can do it! That's for sure. You can make a career with your creativity; you can make what inspires you in the career of your dreams. You need to resist the urge to criticize yourself or judge your ideas. You need to make great plans for yourself. Remember the following quote; if you don't design your own life plan, chances are you'll fall into someone else's plan. And guess what they have planned for you? Not much. Jim Rohn Let this material guide you in your path to success, and use whatever reinforces your motivation to move forward. It doesn't matter where you are at this point on your career; being open, dedicated and focus will help you on your road to succeed. You can find inspiration anywhere you go, so don't forget to always have a pen ready to write any ideas on the blank pages at the back of this book. I will give you simple tips on positive thinking to defeat those negative ones. It's always good to have some quiet time to reflect, re-energize and organize your thoughts. Creative achievement is in your hands, put your heart into it, allow yourself to new adventures, and doors of opportunities will open for you. The sky is the limit! Let's get started, Inner Creative girl!

-Chapter 1-

Let's go girls, Create!

(Even in toughest times)

"Even the most daring and accomplished people
have undergone tremendous difficulty. In fact,
the more successful they became, the more they
attributed their success to the lessons learned during
the most difficult times. Adversity is our teacher.
When we view adversity as a guide towards greater

inner growth, we will then learn to accept the wisdom our soul came into this life to learn."

_Barbara Rose-

$\mathscr{A}$dversity, crisis, and disaster all synonymous of what my soul was facing at the moment, a complete catastrophe. Packing my belongings to catch a flight to Miami, when my future seems a mystery, it was the scariest thought. After months of searching for jobs, struggling paying my rent, and dealing with the consequences of a divorce, I decide to take that drastic decision. It wasn't easy to communicate to my children the big step I was undertaking. They were the only family I had, I felt lonely, and for me real honest friends didn't exist. I got somewhat rebellious; disappointed of people and life. I didn't trust anyone. I know that through the eyes of people I was making the biggest mistake, and in my confusion, doubts, and disorientation it cross my mind too. But among my mistakes I had learned lessons that I won't regret. In Miami I meet the love of my life and that's another story, maybe you might think well she found a rich business men so now all her problems will get solve, not! That wasn't my reality. I meet this wonderful, humble immigrant guy, full of aspirations and unfulfilled dreams and was confronting a life full of hardships and troubles too!!

OMG are you out of your mind!! I know for sure that was the reaction of many, but beyond his situation, I saw a person who values me, hard working men with a full potential ready to unleash. He didn't live in one of Miami's best houses, but his humble way of living make me appreciate more everything about life. When we met I was full of stress and he introduces me to natural remedies that have helped him and his parents. He taught me about the art of calming massages; relaxation techniques, acupressure (which is treatment of symptoms by applying pressure with the fingers to specific pressure points of the body) and many times when I was overwhelm he gently calmed me down with positive words and relaxation music. These techniques were effective for me so I decide to rely more on natural ways to deal with certain ailments. He struggle with money for medication so it was interesting how he came up with natural alternative to live a healthier life style, (by that time I didn't have health insurance either). Food was another struggle, not too much budget for it, but it was just the right portion I need it every day, I start eating only fruits for breakfast and began to notice that I felt more energetic and lighter. Later on, I began reading a detox book that teach me about how adding more fruits to your diet will improve drastically your health, due to the numerous benefits fruits can provide to your system. Eating a simple diet of more fruits and vegetables is a great way to nurture your body with the essential nutrients your body needs to function properly.

The man I meet in Miami became my husband, with him I learned the value of life and he became one of my motivations to the birth of a new passion, natural health. Sometimes just going out for a fresh air or after a great therapeutic message, we took time to have conversations which was relaxing to me. All this activities that we share together make me feel closer, he became my husband my best friend. I recall that I told him that when I was with him I felt a healing touch (I decide to use this name for a program in my developing business). I was conceiving a business, but it wasn't the time just yet to realize it.

Every day I used to cry and suffer the difficult separation of my children while I was at Miami. It was like an emotional roller copter of ups and downs. So I left everything I was doing, which it had nothing to do with the natural health business it was soon to emerge. I pack all my belongings with the hope I was going to see my love again, (it was complicated) I couldn't stand the tears on his eyes as we say goodbye at the airport. But I needed to see my children and fix several issues that were unresolved. I was viewing my life at that moment as a nightmare, I was uncertain of my future and how

I was going to work my way up to provide for my children back in the place where I didn't have any source of support. Back in New Bedford, I first stay at my friend's house, I was afraid because she gave me only one or two weeks to find a place to go. Also because her husband works at night, I had to wake up really early in the morning and find what to do until 5pm. Well, I decide to search for jobs in the morning, complete all my diligences, and go to the library. At the library I spent the rest of the hours until she pick me up. It was one of those days sitting on the dark halls of the library where I start reflecting on my life. While looking around, I saw a book that got my attention, it was called Life shift by Aleta St. James. This book was about a woman that uses natural healing and life coaching skills to motivate people to live to their full potential. The author of the book motivated me because she makes a reality one of her dearest dream, be a mom at the age of 57. After overcoming many obstacles she had beautiful twins. A flash back came to mind, that translate me to my love in Miami, Oh great! I can make a business out holistic and natural health. Besides art I always love the health field but never thought of making a creative business out of it. There were so many branch of the health field it was so hard to choose one that I really love and enjoy. But I narrow down as I knew I was inclining more to prevention due to some work and research of different organizations. I knew I want to focus in woman's health because somehow I was interesting in that field, even though at a young age didn't pay attention to this other inner inclination. But after working as a youth director for so many years, practicing and working in different areas at the church, I finally discover the beauty of the woman's ministry. Overall these experiences and what I learn from my love in Miami I knew that natural health was the perfect field for me. The book I read was only a push to realize my dream and start thinking creatively about my next career move. Each morning got brighter, with the excitement to go to the library and learn more about the new path I was taking. I began to read more books about reflexology, life coaching skills, Therapeutic massages, woman's health, exercise and nutrition. It was one of those days searching for books and reading for so many hours that I had a funny incident. It was kind of funny because after a little exhaustion looking for jobs, a place to live, hours of reading, I couldn't hide how tire I was. And it was one of those tired days that I fell to sleep while I was reading. A librarian approach to me and wake me up by telling me sleeping wasn't allow at the library. This was one of those crazy days that I can't remember without giggle. But after that funny incident at the library, I decide to get up get active and put into practice what

I was learning, so I went for a trip to the gym and learn more about the various exercise programs out there. I took advantage of a promotional offer at a near Gym and got a whole week for free. Plus I got a whole day free at a yoga place called hope. I took all the classes! it was so much fun and at the same time I learned new techniques and new exercise programs like the hip hop yoga class that I love!! Exercising was another stress reliever for me, so when my children were with their dad I went to the gym and exercise. It was complicated not to have an apartment at the beginning because I had to see my kids either at the library or at a Mc Donald's place. My friend told me that her husband was a little uncomfortable with the kids so I couldn't see them at her house that often anymore. It took me a month to find an apartment and move out of my friend's house. I didn't find a good job by that time, so I decide to work for labor ready. Labor ready is a company that helps unemployed people to get a temporary job or a one day job. Every day I woke up at 2am to get ready for work and walk an hour long dark road to get to Labor ready on time. After getting to labor ready I waited like two more hours for them to tell me if I got a job for that day. Thank God, that after waiting those hours I temporarily got an opportunity in a cranberry company from 6am to 6pm in the late afternoon. I was exhausted after that amount of physical activity. It was killing me, waking up at 2am, walking an hour distance every morning and returning home at 7pm or later and sometimes walking the distance back home again because I didn't have a car or money at the moment. The road was pretty scary, I had three horrible experiences as I walk to Labor Ready and in one of those incidents I called the police because I got into a dangerous situation of being followed by men. I couldn't see my kids that much because I need it to work many days and hours in order to provide for them and have them with me. Those where the time when I felt more lonely than ever, couldn't see my kids, my love was so far away, and seeing each other was impossible because his immigrant status at the moment. I didn't trust anyone so I was so lonely. The only thing that kept me going was the desire to keep fighting for my kids; my love in Miami and the emerging career that was taking shape one step at a time. After almost recuperating everything again even a car, disaster strike again when the company I was working for close for a couple of weeks. Couldn't find a job, I was putting my life in danger and everything seeing so awkward for me. I love my children to death but I came to the conclusion that New Bedford wasn't the right place I need it to be, if I wanted to grow as a business woman and provide for them. As a single mom, I discover how difficult it really was to start from zero in your own. After months of struggles, I decide to go back to Miami get the support I needed from people that gain my trust, get married and establish myself to be able to have my children back with me and start my business plan.

I envisioned Miami as a place of opportunity in the area of business, a bright future was awaiting for me. According to a 2009 UBS(Union Bank of Switzerland) study of 73 world cities, Miami was ranked as the richest city in the United States, and the world's fifth-richest city in terms of purchasing power. (from free encyclopedia). It was the perfect place to start because is the major center for finance, commerce, media, entertainment, and the arts!!! Yes the arts! Well, I have a vast range of channels to begin with; a variety of business doors to knock. All my passion were in one place, now was the time to start creating the future I always dream of, using my artistic skills to promote natural health, wellness, and motivate others to fulfill their goals in life.

Discover YOur Passion

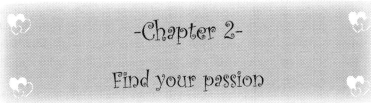

-Chapter 2-

Find your passion

(Become who you are meant to be:
where to start)

You believe and you doubt, you're confused, you
got it all figured out. Everything that you always
wished for, Could be yours, should be yours
if the only knew

—Song "One Step a Time" by Jordan Sparks

&xperiences, that's what it took, many experiences. Disappointments, doubts, failures, mistakes, confusion, obstacles, setbacks, public embarrassment, mess, a total mess! Countless meetings with my friends; the distance of people that I can't live without, including the cutest annoying pet that you got to love; hours of reading in my hidden place, the space where my imagination flow, my bedroom. You name it, and the list can go on and on.

What kept me motivated through all this challenges in life was the motto that I choose for myself; "life challenges are not supposed to paralyze you; they're supposed to help you discover who you are"—Bernice Johnson Reagon—All those challenges became the stepping stones to find myself and discovered my true passion, an avenue for my personal advancement and growth. Your self-fulfillment and growth can't come from getting stuck in your little comfort world, it's something that requires action, and why not, mistakes are allowed along the way, that's perfectly fine, insight will follow. I remember the first step I took to realize what I was capable of doing, it was a day when two of my friends were discussing who were going to make the youth program at the church for the second Friday, opss! it seems no one was up to that challenge that following weekend. I must confess I was newly baptized. I had a bunch of fears, who wouldn't, the first time creating a youth program! OMG, what do I got into! And after seeing the expression of their faces that yelled to me!, are you sure you going to make it? But for some reason I wanted to try it! I was eager to do something, explore ways of doing it, and make it happen. I honestly didn't pay attention to any negative comments; I decide to volunteer my time so it was my responsibility to worked diligently on putting the program together, delegate tasks and asked for help and support when it was necessary. Is never a bad idea to get suggestions from others with experience, in my case, it was my pastor. But it could be any trusted professional in the area you're working on. A word of wisdom from a person who already has the experience is essential to get some feedback and support as you make progress in your project. When the day arrived it was a great success, even though I felt nervous and almost throw up, but I relied on the fact that I worked hard, practice, and make preparation in advance to make this youth program running, yes I was ready. Feeding my mind with those positive thoughts, help me focus in what was really important, sent a message to the young people through the medium I was gifted, the arts. It only took that first initiative to embark on a continuously learning journey, an adventure that each day unfolded new talents and skills. You never stop learning; every day brings you opportunities and the precious gift of time, is your choice to take advantage of it. I'll never forget that first youth program, everyone love it, and congratulate me, like I always say; hard work definitely pays off!

I don't know which step of the ladder you are right now in finding yourself, you could be taking your first baby steps, you might be reaching the top or maybe figuring out how to change directions in your life. Congratulations! If you have this book in your hands you will receive advice not matter what step you're in. At the beginning of this chapter 2, I wrote a portion of one of my favorite songs from Jordin Sparks "One step at a time", you will see it writing further in this book. It emphasize that we all go through up and downs, we all going to experienced confusion at a certain moment in life, we'll embrace the desire to believe but there's going to be times when doubts will fill our minds. But everything that you always whish for, should be yours and will be yours, if they only knew, knew what? who you are! You need to work hard searching for self-identification and start living a motivated life, is then when others will know your value and what you can contribute to the world. If you are self-employ you'll get insight for the quality of service you can deliver or what makes you different from the rest. With a punch of innovation and creativity you can stand out from the competition.

I will give you a quick review with these simple tips to let that inner innovated girl emerge and start your road to success.

TIPS

✓ Face your fears: Your worst enemy is your fears; by conquering them it will be easier to explore your passion. It could be that you care too much about a possible failure or it could be something else that you giving too much emphasis. Finding ways to cope with your fears will be an important process that will lead you to your passion.

✓ Be open to new experiences: Many people have a hard time getting out of the comfort zone and opt for a monotonous way of life, doing the same thing every single day. If you haven't found out who you are just yet, it won't come as magic act. You need to take new challenges because you never know where life is going to take you. Have you ever try something that you where to afraid of? I gave you my example when I first took the initiative to create a youth program for the first time! What if you decide to do something different each day?

✓ Make an inventory of your talents: There was a connection between my passion for art and other skills I acquire working as a youth director in my church. That connection continues today, by using my theatrical talents when I'm doing speaking engagement, seminars or programs to get my message out. Everyone has an especial talent or hobby. You don't have to be an expert right now. You can decide to take it to a higher level and make it your passion. Ask yourself these questions, Can you become an expert? Can you make a profession out it? Can you write about it?

✓ Let people support you: Don't be embarrass to ask for support. We are here to help each other out. By opening your trust to family, friend and colleagues it could take you a step closer in realizing what you always wanted, also giving them the opportunity to feel needed. Asked as many questions as you can, it may help you make up your mind.

✓ Gather information: research for topics on subjects you enjoy the most, try every medium you can, books, magazines articles or the internet. Practice all the skills you learn and start developing your passion.

✓ Accept Mistakes: Allow yourself to try new things even when you're not 100% sure it will succeed. Often you'll come across with different strategies or better alternatives along the way.

✓ Get inspire by other ideas: There's thousands of ways of making something look different. Use your innovated ideas to created in your unique point of view

✓ Never give up: Your path to success it may not be easy; but don't let anything interfere in your path to success. Remind yourself every day that nothing will stop you on achieving you ultimate goal

Remember to stick to a plan, is not enough to dream or talk about who you want to become, it requires more than that action yes action you need to visualize the life that you always want it and start living it! Take the necessary actions to achieve it. Once you know where you headed, keep yourself motivate every day.

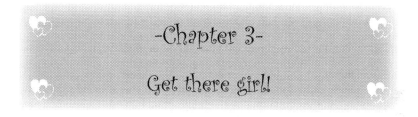

-Chapter 3-

Get there girl!

"Formal education will make you a living,
but self-education will make you a fortune"

Jim Rohn

*I*f you want to know where you are capable to
go in your journey to success, I will share with you
an important lesson I learned while working as a

youth leader. We learn most in life by taking action, but there is an effective way to grow as a person each day, reading, reading, reading, learning, learning, and practicing; readers are leaders! In my opinion what Jim Rohn mean by "fortune" in his quote is the valuable character development a person acquires that no money can't buy. The riches knowledge can bring to you and the life of others. By taking the time each day to read and learn something new, we are not only enriching our life with knowledge but the life of others too. Formal education is wonderful, but we need to keep "digging deeper", beyond those school years. It took me a lot of time to adapt to a college life, and to choose a career path that was a good fit for me. I remember how lost I felt at the beginning in the college world. I was so disoriented; I needed some sort of direction as where I was going. I face many consequences by not getting or searching for that guide immediately. I navigate in a college world without knowing where my final destination was. Headaches, all I got after taking classes that I didn't even need it for my program of study. And that was just a portion of what happen; it took a few withdrawn from classes which was a waste of money and time. A road trip that was normally two years, it took me six! Well, those years includes a few experimental jobs, volunteer work at church and being a dedicated mom of four! When you are lost if you don't quickly seek for some sort of guide is going to be a struggle to find your final destination. After learning step by step how to correctly navigate the college world I start to make some progress. But it was a mixture of college experiences with the volunteer work at church (practice) plus my desire of self-growth (digging deep into books) influence important career decisions during my college life. It wasn't after all those years volunteering, working with people at different church departments, and all those life experiences to discover my true career path. Today I can say without a doubt that I'm finally in love with my career choice. The important lesson here is search, learn, and practice. It is imperative to know ourselves, our goals and where we heading in life. Is a process that requires continuing learning, practice, acquire skills for a desire outcome. Below I will provide you with some tips that will help you in your road trip to success!

✓ Keep yourself motivated, I hear once that motivation is momentaneous, but I think is like taking a shower, to keep yourself clean you need to take a shower daily, also to keep yourself motivated you have to make it an everyday activity.

✓ Get to know your strengths by self-evaluation and evaluation from others you can trust, and work in your area of interest. Don't get discourage or take any advice personal, but take advantage and improve those areas you need it the most. (you will find your talent evaluation questions further on this chapter) Leaders can't take criticism personally, remember that leaders need to withstand criticism and overcome obstacles.

✓ If you are attracted by a career path, certain qualities, or strategies from a person you admire, find out how they achieve their success and follow their path. It's likely that if you are attracted to certain qualities of your role model is because you can see in action the qualities that need to develop within yourself. Polish those qualities. Then create the best version of yourself!

✓ Volunteer at an organization that you might be interested in. Get to learn as much you can about your field. Start your way of building a killer portfolio of your work.

✓ Sharpen your skills continually; you may think you are the best at what you do. And that could be right. But the truth is, we never stop learning, every day we learn something new. Is substantial for any career to keep improving the skills you already have and add new ones to your list. Sharpening your skills can bring great benefits for your career. Professionally, it will take you as far of the game you want and keep you on top. It will get you better projects, clients, salary, and a great reputation. Who doesn't want that? Personal growth is important in any type of business because it keeps you challenge, interested, alive and passionate about what you do. Without any challenges any job will become boring and tiresome. But if you constantly look for ways to improve what you do, there's not going to be a chance for an unexcited moment!

✓ Do yourself a reality check and answer these questions; how passionate are you about what you do or want to do? How dedicated and committed are you? now that your turn those talents into a career path you need to manage to work on both, the creative and business aspects of it. You need to visualize yourself working all day, every single day! Are you ready for this challenge, is a big responsibility specially if you going to be your own boss, but at the same time it rewarding, think about it. At least you need to commit 8 hours of your day and maybe some extra overtime hours to make it work.

That's something that requires a lot of discipline, energy and passion!

✓ Find a mentor that inspires you and you can learn from. Start building relationships with people with knowledge in the different areas that can enrich your career. I had an English professor that was really good at teaching, she wrote many publications and it was involved in many publishing activities. I admire her because her class was very interesting and she almost persuades me to go for a creative writing career. But writing alone wasn't my passion, but I sure do enjoy it, and appreciate everything I learn from her. She was always available if I needed some sort of advice other than a homework assignment!

TALENT SELF-EVALUATION

The topics I'm most interesting in are:

_____

_____

The hobbies and activities I enjoy the most and lose track of time are:

_____

_____

If I volunteer my time in a creative company or organization will be_____

_____ the skills I will like to acquire from this experience will be_____

_____

Having a conversation with professional

_____ He/she told me my talent and abilities were

_____

_____

When I asked professional

_____ what skills I need to posses or improve or what action steps I needed to take in order to make a living out of

_____

their response was

_____

_____

To be able to become a _____
I must take the following trainings_____

_____

In my honest opinion I need to improve in the following abilities or areas in my life

_____

_____

I plan to grow and improve by

_____

_____

I'm taking _____ of my time to sharpen my skills and learn new ones

By the end of the year, I want my level of skills to be

_____

_____

Girls that make it happen!

The Female entrepreneur Association is a great website that motivates entrepreneur girls out there through real life stories of woman that work their way up to be their own boss. While reading different articles, I came across two great stories of success that caught my attention. The first article I read was about a woman that use to see herself as always depressed, hated exercise, she was falling into an overeating precipice while experiencing poor self esteem and frustration. But after realizing the unhealthy path her life was taking she decides to take control of her negative thoughts and feelings and change her life completely. After taking that positive determination her life took a drastic turn and now she is known as the fat controller. She motivate people to stay fit, happy stronger and avoid myth about diets and exercise. She runs a thirty minute fat-burning class call Fitstop, monthly cooking courses and online fat-loss programs for people all over the country. One of her biggest challenges was believe in herself. She was challenged to develop and polish her skills in areas such as Public speaking, networking, marketing, but that was obstacles that she overcomes with a lot of practice and dedication. She was determined not to give up and as I mention before asking for help was one of the action she took to achieve success. I relate to the advice she gave to other business girls, to do only what you're passionate about otherwise it won't feel like a job. I have a similar quote everywhere even on my face book! I love to hear and read motivational stories of how people overcome obstacles and took the initiative to achieve great success. It makes me stronger each day. Another story that I want to share with you was about another woman that was facing some personal challenges and a divorce. She needed to get back up financially, but she saw those problems as an opportunity to grow and take a new path in her life. Since she grew up in a family environment that used natural plants as remedies and prepared natural beauty products, which became her source of motivation to begin her training in the field of aromatherapy and massage therapy. She also started developing natural products that were gentle to the environment and the skin. She set up an online shop for all her product and start promoting her business through social media. Her advice for woman that are starting a business was to connect to your local network groups, take advantage of any local business developing programs which are a great for starters because those programs offer network opportunities, workshops on different topics and support for small business. There's a lot of woman out there with great success stories that inspires us every day and the good news is that you can be one of them!

Nothing is impossible; the word itself says 'I'm possible! Audrey Hepburn

POSITIVE ENERGY GIRL!

Girl, there's a challenging journey ahead of you, stay focus and develop a positive attitude everyday by:

✓ Having a moment to feel grateful for something in your life, it will give you a sense of satisfaction and a motivation to keep moving! You can be thankful for having a place to sleep, having food to eat, for the things that God has giving you the opportunity to do and accomplish. Being thankful put you in a position of appreciation and receiving. This way you're developing a positive attitude that will help you deal with future life challenges. Here's my list: God's help in my life, my Children, my wonderful husband and His mom, soon becoming a certified exercise instructor, even my mistakes because of the good lessons learn. Make your list!

✓ Look at negative past experiences as learning tool you can use to inspire others. Think of at least one positive thing you got out of a challenging situation in your past, that way you'll archive personal growth, and it will be easier to find something good out of your next life challenges. If you deal with your first challenge in a positive way you already obtained all the necessary tools to overcome the next challenge. Remember, that everything bad that happens to us has also a positive side.

✓ Develop the skill to talk to yourself in a positive way. "I m doing good" "I'm confident" "I'm a hard worker" "I'm achieving great things" Allow yourself to experience the great feeling of that positive energy throughout your body. You're a valuable person and you deserve great things to come to your life. Praise yourself for all the hard work and the accomplishments you're making. You don't need to wait for someone else to tell you this, you can tell yourself every single day!

✓ Boost your self-esteem by acknowledging something difficult or important that you manage to accomplish. It could be obtaining a degree, creating a magazine, or speaking to hundreds of people, it could be anything! Take note of those positive qualities that help you with achievement. It could be Leadership, determination, persistence, ect. Good news to feel wonderful about, you posses those qualities, love yourself and bring those qualities into action anytime! You go girl!

✓ Don't lose focus of your main goal. Focusing on your main goal give you a sense of direction, purpose and self-fulfillment. Keeping yourself busy on that goal will lead you to maintain a positive state of mind.

✓ Read positive quotes: "Just when a caterpillar thought the world was over, it became a butterfly" Author Unknown I like to place them everywhere to have a piece of inspiration all the time.

✓ Smile everyday! is good for your body is good for your health!

✓ Help someone: You can perform all this things at once. Help a person, develop new skills by helping that person and experience the joy of fulfilling a need, that way you take your mind away of your negative thoughts and focus your energy on others.

Sing. Singing make you feel better! and of course is something I love to do, There's a song that became one of my favorites, every time I listen to it, brings a dose of motivation to my life, I mentioned before is "One Step At a Time" by Jordan Sparks

SOMETHING TO REMEMBER

Watch your thoughts, they become words.
Watch your words, they become actions.
Watch your actions, they become habits.
Watch your habits, they become your character.
Watch your character, it becomes your destiny.
Happy positive thinking!

Welcome

Carol Ramos

Chapter 4

Self-employed: Girl on fire

"Positive belief in yourself will give you the energy needed to conquer the world and this belief is the power behind all creation."

—<u>Stephen Richards</u>

𝒜fter years working as a youth leader, my own learning experiences and challenges, I finally decide to take a big step in my life and become an entrepreneur girl. It was those challenges that make me stand stronger and gave me the motivation and a burning desire to do something satisfying and at the same time provide for my children. Motivation is the reason I keep moving forward, seeing myself at the level I want to be as a professional and trust in my abilities to make difficult decisions to make it happen. I know what I want. Now that I got my goals, talents, skills and a big idea in place; I envision working for myself. There's nothing more satisfying than waking up in the morning with the satisfaction that I'm working hard every day to accomplish my own aspirations. Being self-employed sounds glamorous, but in reality to experience great success and satisfaction it takes a special kind of person. It takes a person that is motivated, dedicated, and discipline to climb the ladder of success. I have my bad days, but the majority of my time is spent working hard to achieve my goals and exercise those three major traits in my life. I know that being self-employed is hard work, but for me doing hard work that I enjoy versus working on something I hate the rest of my life is a fair trade-off. I have to put in long hours to my developing business project, so I decide to downside my current full-time job to be able to achieve my goals for this year. I know is a big decisions, but if you have faith in your project you need to take risk! When Thomas Edison was interviewed by a young reporter who asks him boldly if he felt like a failure or if he ever thought of giving up, I was so inspired by his strong leadership response. Edison replied, "Young man, why would I feel like a failure? And why would I ever give up? I now, know definitively over 9,000 ways that an electric light bulb will not work. Success is almost in my grasp." And shortly after that, and over 10,000 attempts, Edison invented the light bulb. That's an attitude that should characterize every leader today. Today's leaders will succeed by developing that passion, commitment and dedication to hard work. Fortunately, working in the field of holistic health and nutrition with a focus on woman's health, it doesn't feel like work to me. Mainly because is what I love doing and I have the opportunity to use my inner creative side and abilities to make it more excited, so I can't complain! It definitely takes courage to stand up for yourself and do what you always dream of doing; willing to take action with no guarantees of success. Willing to put all your heart and soul to an enterprise that you work so hard to overcome any obstacles because is your commitment is your passion. Every self-employed person needs to take courage and responsibility to create the life and business they always wanted. It's about challenging yourself and the world. This was the desire I had within me all the time; it just took several steps to realize it! All my life I try a few jobs in different organization but always my soul was screaming for something more, I love certain aspects of each job that I had but the pieces of the puzzles weren't in place at that moment. There was a piece missing all the time. Even when I was in college, something was missing, many careers but I wanted a career that that covers all the areas I love working and that I can put into action all my acquire skills. From each work experience, I evaluated what enjoy the most doing, for example, when I developed a youth program each week, the best part for me was organizing it, looking for participants, speaking in public. I got better each time I practice, and then I look for ways to improve them for the next event. So, now those past experiences lead me to my dream career today. This is what my inner creative girl was looking for all this time, a career that gathers all my creative skills, my passion for woman's health and leadership. Self-evaluation was important to me at the conclusion of each program because it gave me a feedback of how I was doing and what areas I need improvement. Another important skill for me is people skills because I was dealing with people all the time and it was something I enjoyed. Providing some sort of support to them was at the top of my career list. Building rapport and understanding them is a step to success in any career path, we always dealing with people on a certain level, either by phone if you are a customer service representative or personal contact, but the rule is always the same, delivering the best quality customer service will definitely help your business flourish. Is important to have people skills to deal with their unique personalities and any kind of situation that might arise, there's no way around it! Before starting any program my focus was to make everyone that walk through the doors of the church feel welcome and care for. I was always waiting for them with a great smile, a warm welcome and hand shake. Establishing good relationship with your customers it got to be a top priority in any type of business. You definitely got to be a people person when thinking of being your own boss.

Here's a list of other characteristics an entrepreneur girl should strive to develop or maintain if you want your business off the ground!

✓ Save Money!—Every beginning is difficult, tell me about it! I know that us woman dream or die for those gorgeous shoes we saw at the last trip to the mall. But now that we are at this level of making an enterprise grow saving is a plus and so it is having an excellent credit and relationship with your bank. I learn this the hard way, but I got to say I'm getting way better with my spending habits. Going through a divorce make me realize how hard life is when you're in your own. The weight of paying all the bills, working long hours, then providing for your children is challenging for every woman. It becomes very hard to manage everything by yourself. But it was those moments that taught me how important was to watch out for my spending habits, so I work on a tight budget to be able to get everything I need it. Another thing you need to take charge is your credit, after a divorce my credit wasn't that pretty and at this moment I'm still working hard to get my credit back into excellent shape, is a lot of work and you might experience frustration but is fundamental for every business. Challenging times are going to come but as an entrepreneur girl you need to be willing to take responsibility for the good, the bad and the ugly side of your business. It is important to begin with a rock start financial stability before thinking of anything else. It takes a lot of sacrifice at the beginning, maybe you might need to forget about those gorgeous shoes for now, but I'm pretty sure that your business look better on you that those shoes any time. It will pay off at the end. See yourself as a confident entrepreneur leader; trust your knowledge and abilities to make difficult decisions. Move on!

✓ Know that your thinking like an entrepreneur make plans and prepared yourself to make your business succeed and flourish. A business success doesn't come by chance but is the result of your concentrated effort.

✓ Remember that you can't do it all! If you need help making your products and services unique from the rest, gain management experience, need more financial assistance, ask for help. There are many resources today that can help you succeed! Entrepreneur's girls take advantage of any resources available, so her time can be well spent on crucial issues that need to be prioritized. Here is a list of organizations that can help your business grow!

✓ SCORE (Service Corps of Retired Executives) Is a non-profit association that is dedicated to educate entrepreneurs to built, grow and make your small business succeed nationwide. This Score Association is comprised of volunteers that serve as "counselors" to America's small business. Retired, working executives and business owners volunteer their time and knowledge to provide confidential counseling support and mentoring. The great part is that is completely free!

✓ Small Business Meet-ups: Find local business meet-up groups. It's a great way to find customers, connect to other helpful organizations, get advice and hear other people overcome business barriers and achieved great success. Search for Small Business Meet-ups groups type your Country and zip code and press search choose the best for you!

✓ Local Chamber Of Commerce: Is a great place to network, establish relationships with other entrepreneurs, educational workshops and seminars. Find your local Chamber Of Commerce and start getting your business notice in your community. I decide to be a member of the Woman's Chamber Of Commerce of Miami Dade because since my focus will be on woman is a great start for me.

✓ Social Media Group: This is a vital resource for your developing business. With this new technological era is important to have knowledge of all kind of social media and how it will assist your business with marketing efforts. Is a great opportunity to create, share, interact or exchange ideas in virtual communities and networks.

✓ SBA (Small Business Administration): Is a United States organization that provides support to entrepreneurs and small business. The government has provided local resources across the states to better assist small business development. You can find all sort of information and resources that are helpful and anything related to your business. It also provides online training and resources to start developing your business plan.

✓ American Express Open Forum: American express is a great informative site geared towards entrepreneurs and small business. This company has put together useful tools and resources in their online forum that keep entrepreneurs girls like me coming back for more. They discuss topics such as sales, management, financing, marketing and interesting articles that give you creative ideas for your business. You can use the site as a non-member and access the information available in the site but if you desire more interaction you need to have an America Express card and become a member. By becoming a member you can be an active online community member, participate on their discussion, forums and make comments on important business blogs. I found this website very helpful and the articles were interesting full of useful ideas for your business and marketing efforts.

✓ Startup Nation: This a great site for entrepreneurs and business owners. It provides a lot of resources for entrepreneur's mom, successful business moms and business in general. There are a lot of valuable information, articles, ideas and the community is there to support your efforts to make your "great idea" into a "great business". There's contest like the Leading Moms in Business Competition to support woman that are moms and business owners!

✓ Business.Gov: This is a great federal government small business resource website. You can find information and support on how to start your business, writing your business plan, financing, managing employees, marketing, taxes, loans, grants, and more. You can get connected to other business owners and take advantage of programs and services available to get your business started. You can find them in social media like twitter, LinkedIn, facebook and at www.business.Gov

✓ Entrepreneur.com: In this website you can find the business news and articles, expert's advice, growth strategies for small business owners. You can also get the latest business information by subscribing to the Entrepreneur business magazine.

All this organizations and groups offer a variety of resources, expertise and support for small business. The only way it can work for you is by taking advantage of its programs and services and take an active role that will lead you to succeed. Keep helpful contact information on a business organizer designated just for networking contacts. Get connected with other social media such as LinkedIn or twitter and find out the latest news on like-minded small businesses. Keep all your profiles up-to-date and with current information of the what's new and excited in your business.

You could make
a **wish**
or you can make it happen

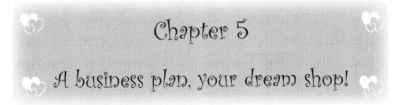

Chapter 5

A business plan, your dream shop!

There is no royal, flower-strewn path to success.
And if there is, I have not found it. For if I have
accomplished anything in life, it is because I have
been willing to work hard.

—*C.J. Walker*

$\mathcal{I}$ know that just the thought of a lengthy time consuming business plan can intimidate you, but a business plan is crucial for visualize where your heading. A business plan is a written description of the future of your business. It's a document that will give insight of what you're planning to do and how you going to make it happen. let's think about running your business like taking that wonderful trip you always dream about. You have envisioned a great destination for your business, now is important to make the necessary plans and preparations to make this trip the most pleasant one. Your business plan is like all those necessary preparations and plans you are making for you big trip! *When I was a youth leader, I decide to build a non-profit organization which I name Link2life. The purpose of this organization was to promote healthy behaviors in teens through the arts. I began to search for different grants for my organization and I found the perfect one. Then came the difficult part, the proposal! I didn't have a clue on how to write a proposal so I hire someone to do it for me. I gain a lot of valuable experience in this process and for me is pretty similar to a business plan. I was in constant communication with the grant writer and in the process I wrote like ten job descriptions in collaboration with him. After finishing my proposal I wanted to learn more so I went to my local community development clinic and took a grant proposal workshop. I know is hard work, many questions, but it can be done.*

In psychology there's a theory known as the left-brain or right-brain dominance. According to this theory a "left-brained" person is said to be more logical, analytical or sequential. On the other hand, a "right-brained" person is more artistic, creative, imaginative, and see the bigger picture. The fact is that while some of our traits may lean more to a specific side of the brain, we are a mix of them both. For us Inner creative girls writing a business plan might sound like a hassle especially if we tend to lean more to the right brain thinking. I like to use my right brain more than the left brain but when it comes to business is good to exercise both side of the brain in order to be more successful in our business life. The idea is to exercise both side of the brain to increase innovation and obtain optimal results in anything we do. I'm creating my business plan using the "traditional format" with Growthink' Ultimate Business Plan Template. This software is a great resource for beginners; it will get you started and guide you step by step to a successful business plan. With this template you can create your business plan in eight hours if you already have covered your business basics. Is simple, easy to use, and will generate the results you are looking for in a *shorter period of time. This is what I call exercising my left side of the brain. Also I'm sharing with you a creative approach to start coming out with ideas for your business plan. I call it the Inner creative girl visualize-Action guide for success. This guide will get you started with a visual summary of what your business plan is all about. I call it visualize-Action because after you had created your own visual guide for your business plan you can use it as a reference tool for your "traditional" business plan. Having a clear vision of what you want to achieve in your business is crucial for creating your reality. Creating a visualize-Action guide can help you get from where you are now to where you want to be. This will make a mental picture of your business come to live. Why? By looking through magazines images you will realize what you really want and what you don't and it will bring more focus to what you want to accomplish. It's a great idea to place your visualize-Action guide where you can look at it every day to help you remind you of the dreams and goals you're aiming for. Visualizing wouldn't be enough you need to set goals for yourself and make a plan of action. To make it easy for you, I'm going to divide the business plan essentials into three sections. This sections include; **Analysis** (Company, Industry, Customers, competition, market) **Action Plan** (Marketing & Sales, Operations, Management team)*

Projections *(Financial plan & business future). I'm going to cover a summary of all steps in a business plan. Remember it's just a summary visualization of the Executive summary on a "traditional business plan". This page is crucial because is your big opportunity to wow your investors. You are going to need to expand each step with more information and data in your "traditional business plan".*

But first, I want you to think of your business as a Star Business no matter how big or small your company is visualize it as number one, as the best of the best! name or rename your big idea, get a name that capture the attention of your audience that draw a lot of interest and make people excited when they hear the story behind it. What is your Star business stage name? Remember be bold, a glam company needs a star name. Think of a attractive name, it doesn't have to make sense but it needs to inspire interest right away. Express yourself and be free spirit! Use a name that reflects what you do. Once you have decide what name you want to give to your star business go and reserve it as a domain name. When I tough of Inner Creative Girl I was also thinking of brand extensions such as Creationgirl cosmetics, ICreativegirl coaching this is just examples of different projects where you can use your brand name. Now that we emphasize a little the importance of your Brand's name let's get started with a step by step example of the Inner

Creative Girl Visualize-Action guide to success! The first step of our summary will be a brief description of your company, what you do?

Make this part of your summary shine is what is going to get the attention of potential investors! Here is an example to guide you.

Example: *Inner Creative Girl offers Life Coaching, Health and wellness programs for woman eighteen and up with a holistic approach that adopt the whole-person wellness model focusing on the* *four dimensions of health—physical, emotional/ intellectual, social and spiritual important to obtain a balance healthy life style.*

*Your Brand's description and all this questions that you can observe in this illustration is part of your **business Analysis** (Company, Industry, Customers, competition, market). We are done with your brand's description which represents who you are as a business entity, now we are going to focus on the other section of the **Business Analysis** in this case your customers.*

***Example:** Our customers are woman eighteen and up who choose a holistic approach to enrich their lives and are looking for a facility that adopt* *a whole-person wellness model to maintain that balance healthy lifestyle they are aiming for. Inner Creative Girl offers a multidimensional programming, services and products that will help our customers develop a more balance life style and make their health and fitness a priority.*

*As you can see on the above example I pretty much answer in a short paragraph who is my customer? What is the need of the customer? And what I can offer to them? Know let's take a look of the **industry** and **Market** that includes **competitors and** we will be done with the section **Analysis***

Example: Across Miami the health and wellness business has seen an explosion of growth over the last x years. Miami is an affluent are with a high density of health and wellness enthusiast. Our market research has shown that x percent of woman prefer a holistic approach for their overall well-being

Here's is another example of how your business will stand out

Example: While there are currently x amount of businesses offering Health & wellness programs in Miami only x amount of these offer part of the services we provide and none focus on the multidimensional program we offer.

*Now that we finish the basics for the **Analysis** section of your business plan, let's focus on the **Action Plan** Section*

Marketing is a vital and important strategy for your business success. Don't just focus on the creation of a brand but start thinking creatively and cultivate a "fanatical group" of consumer that will follow you from now and beyond. Create passionate "fans" eager to buy your products, services or anything related to you! Become a famous entity by your inspiring message and built your community around that massage. Focus on your highly engage "fans" and work with those "super-fans" who will spread the word about you, your services and products. Lead with values and create good relationships and emotional connection with your "followers" by presenting what you believe. Dare to give your fans a name, I want to call all my "fans" Inner creative girls because I know that there's a lot *of potential in each one of us. A name will give your customers a sense of belonging and self-identity as part of a group. The important factor is not to forget about your "fans" the people that make your business grow. Become their "fans" too and make them feel special and important. Give your fans something worthy to talk about, make your business a reason to constantly talk about you! Be bold and design your website, blog or any other social media pages that speak boldly from your heart. Who are your glam business stars? Who are those super star companies that inspire you and that you admire the most? Study them, take notes and add your own touch. When you are thinking about a product, service or anything pretending to your business, think about it like everything coming together to tell a great story. That will be a fantastic way to wow your fans and make them comeback for more. Make your goal to be one of the most influential person in the world! How do you do that? Work hard on polishing your skills and cultivating your talents, give back to the world and never give up. It's about taking radical actions and going beyond what's expected from you to stand out from the crowd.*

*Here is the example from the **Action plan** section (marketing)*

Example: Inner Creative Girl marketing strategy is to emphasize the quality of services we provide and the availability of our services. Costumers will be happy that we help them achieve greater health and minimize medical problems.

This will be an example of staff needed for services

Example: All services given by the Inner Creative girl center will be provided by staff trained in the health and wellness field. On startup we will have x amount of trained staff and expected to hire x more.

★COMING ATTRACTIONS★

YOUR PROGRAMS.EVENTS SERVICES.PRODUCTS

Example: The management team of the Inner Creative Girl Center consist of

_____, _____,
_____, _____

X person has extensive experience in health and wellness while x person worked in sales & marketing for x amount of years. In addition we have put together a board of advisors to provide management expertise. The advisors are x people.

Stellar Profit & Brand's Future
Financial and Projections

#1

Expected Revenue
Expected expenses

Brand's Future

Dont's for my Business
1.   2.   3.

Positive Actions to Continue in my Business
1.   2.   3.
Immediately actions I need to take

1.   2.   3.

This will be an example of the last section of your business plan the **Financials & projections**

Example: Based on the size of our market our sales projections for the first year are x amount of money. The salary for each staff and owner is x amount of money. We are seeking an operating line of x amount of money to finance our first year of growth. We have invested x amount of money. We see a positive future for our business we already have service commitment from over x amount of costumers. A strategy that had work in our business is the aggressively mass media campaigns and a variety of onsite multidimensional events, programs and activities. All the service that the Inner Creative girl Center will provide is sure to appeal every woman in the Miami area.

Now that we reviewed the important sections of a business plan with the above summary you can start

getting into action and create your own Visualize—Action business plan book. This set will include all the craft materials you will need with step by step instructions on how to get started with your rock star business vision! It's like having a Pinterest board of your business vision.

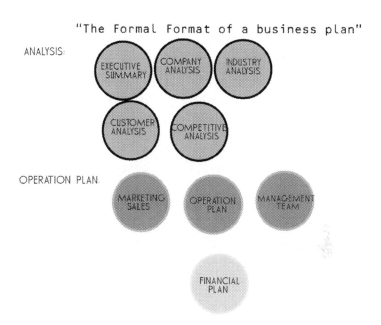

"The Formal Format of a business plan"

ANALYSIS:

EXECUTIVE SUMMARY — COMPANY ANALYSIS — INDUSTRY ANALYSIS

CUSTOMER ANALYSIS — COMPETITIVE ANALYSIS

OPERATION PLAN:

MARKETING SALES — OPERATION PLAN — MANAGEMENT TEAM

FINANCIAL PLAN

Executive Summary: As I mentioned before, *this part of your summary needs to shine because is what is going to get the attention of potential investors! The Executive Summary summarizes each section of the entire business plan. However, it should be the last section you write since is a summary of the entire document. Yet, is the first section that appears in your business plan. A brief description of your business is included in your Executive summary but you have to describe your company in greater detail later in your company's description section. Remember, all this process is part of Analysis which includes company, industry, customers, competition and market. I'm going to review each one of those in great detail but let's continue with what you need in your executive summary.*

- ✓ A brief description of your company(we discussed that above)
- ✓ You need to add your mission, vision and values statements

What is a mission statement? A mission statement should address three essential components; **Key market**: Who is your target customer? **Contribution**: what product or service you will provide to your customer? And **Distinction**: What make your product/service unique from the rest? Why should the customer choose you?

Example: Inner Creative Girl provides women eighteen and older state-wide a holistic multidimensional approach to health that will help them obtain an optimum healthy life style.

Key market: Provides woman eighteen and older state-wide

Distinction: a holistic multidimensional approach to health

Contribution: that will help them obtain an optimum healthy life style

What is a value statement: A value statement will express what your company's believes are.

A vision statement answers the question where. Where is your company headed?

In the Executive Summary section you going to write the whole plan but in a shorter and precise version like the Vizualize-Action example we reviewed earlier. This section should be left for last since is a repetition of the entire plan.

Let's take a look at the **Company Analysis:** In this section of your business plan you need to add your business basic information such as mission,values, vision statements. It is important to include the history of your company and products or services the company sells. If the company is a manufactoring company what type of products does it makes? What is the demand for those products? On the other hand if your company is a service company what type of services will you provide?

Industry Analysis: In this section of your business plan it is important to understand what is going on in your industry as a whole. Is the industry new,expanding, stable or declining? If your industry is "growing" for example you company have a good advantage here. What gives your business a competitive advantage? This section also analize economic factors, supply and demand, competitors,future situations, technology, legal and political factors.

Customers Analysis: In order for your business to be succesful you need to know who is going to buy your products or services and how your company is going to meet your customers specific needs. You need to include the demographic of your customers including their age, occupation, spending habits, ect. Consider their behavior to trends,technology, price and decide how you will aproach them.

Competitive analysis: This section describe who your competitors are and what does the industry looks like.What are their strengths and weakenesses, what make you stand out from them or what set you apart. Also it help you identify what are your potential opportunities and threats in the market.

All this sections that we just reviewed are part of your **Analysis** in your business plan. Each section needs detail explanation and research that you can find in government agencies,U.S. census Bureau or industry associations.

Know let's take a look of The Action planning sections of your business plan that include: **Marketin plan & sales, Operation plan and Management Team**

Marketing plan & sales: This section explain what your marketing stragety will be, how you will execute such a plan and how you are going to generate sales. You need to ask yourself the following questions:

Who is your target market? How will you brand your company? How does this image is going to help you connect with your target audience? What methods are you using to reach your customers? How you are going to Advertise your company? How much will it cost? Where you potential customers get the product or services you are selling? How will you offer a superior product or service?

Operation Plan: This section will describes how your company works and how all task and procedures will be carry out. This is important not only to your investors but to you, to your management team and your employees. The operational plan includes the following:

Where your business will be located? What is the advantages or disadvantages of the area? How will you counteract the negatives? If this is aplicable to you, is important to know who is going to be your suppliers/vendors,how will you manage your inventory. How your production and distribution process will work? How will you sell your product or service? Who your staff will be? What job they are going to perform? What policies or proceduress do you have in place for your company?

Management team: You need to provide the legal structure of your company in this section and introduce all of the business owners. If you are the sole proprietor or there's multiple owners. You need to adress each person's education background and experience related to the businness. What percentage of ownership each person has and what's their contribution within the company. You need to include job descriptions, resume, credetials, payment and any other related information.

All this sections belongs to the **Action plan** of your business plan, know let's focus in the last section which is going to cover the financial plan & projections

Financial Plan: This section opf your plan should include three key financial statements: Income,balance and cash flow statements.

Income statement: This stament summarizes your business's revenue and expenses.

Balance sheet: This show your business's assets and liabilities

Cash Flow: This shows how much money you expect to be coming in and out of your business in a certain time frame.

The financial plan will tell investors where you stand in the present time financially, what's your financial history been like and where is your business standing in the future financially.

If you're a new business your statements can be tentative but you can make it realistic by looking at similar business financial reports that has been published. If this is not you area of expertise you can always hire a financial professional to do the job for you.

Smart Performance Goal				
strategies how i will achive the goal?	Action Steps my to do list	Lead Role/ Resources Needed	Target Date	Date Completated
1				
2				
3				

Take Action entrepreneur girl!

Something to remember is that when you take ACTION, everything gets done. When you just have a great idea or vision but you don't take any action towards the goal then there nothing to get done. It's great to have a vision, goals, positive self-talk like I mention on a previous chapter, but none of that will be important unless you make the decision to take action toward what you want to achieve! So keep moving creative girl!

OPENING YOUR DREAM SHOP!

Productivity is never an accident. It is always the result of a commitment to excellence, intelligent planning, and focused effort.

—*Paul J. Meyer*

Now let's focus on creating your own working environment. When opening your own shop, location is an important aspect to take into consideration. The environment you create for yourself and your customers are key for business success. If you start working from home like me, create a wonderful environment for you workplace. It could be a comfortable space in your own room or other place where you can feel comfortable and can concentrate in your work. Decorate in a way that is inspiring for you and motivate you to wakeup everyday and get to work. Get a punch of colors that will inspire your creativity, your vision and to reach your full potential. On the other hand if you have already an establishment try to think about how you space will be more attractive to your customers and make them come back to your store.

I have research a lot of stores and observe how they promote their services, showcase their products and deliver services. For my surprise I have visited establishments that look so good on the outside, posses a nice location, great décor but when you walk inside the store the poor showcase of their product, poor customer service and dissorganization make you walk right out. When opening a shop you need keep in mind that is your image you're selling, you got to make your space shine! It requires planning and some research. Opening the shop that you always dream of involves looking for demographics, suppliers, examining your competition, staying on budget, having an understanding of laws and taxes, and the list can go on. Here are some factors to consider when opening your dream shop:

- ✓ Parking Space—Find a location that could offer parking space for your customers, a shop with parking space is a shop with more possibilities of customer's traffic!
- ✓ Brand Image—what is the image you want to promote? Is it compatible with the location you choose for your business?

✓ Competition—What can make you stand out from your competitors is quality service, top customers service, good prices, ect.

✓ Plan for future growth—look for space your company can growth when its ready

✓ Zoning regulations—will determine whether or not you can conduct your business in certain properties or locations. To find out more contact your local planning agency

✓ Evaluate your finances—Hidden cost like renovation, decorating, Technology upgrades, and other cost. Also be aware about the income, sales and property taxes rate in your state.

✓ Check the Department of Labor for a list of minimum wages rate by state

✓ Do your homework and learn more about Government Economic Incentives—Maybe your business location can qualify for government economic business programs, such as state-specific small business loan and other financial incentives

✓ Is the location your choose business friendly?—There's a many government organization as I mention earlier that help small businesses start up and succeed. Organizations such as SBA Offices, Small Business Development Clinics, Woman's Business Centers and other government-funded programs can help you in journey to success!

Building your Business presence

In order to build a good business presence your business needs to be visible to your community and start developing good relationships with local leaders and neighbors. Is a great idea to constantly promote your business and get involved in community events and local organizations.

✓ Take advantage of social groups and networks to promote your business, face book, twitter, you tube. All this social groups are great places to build a fan base, provide you with customer service feedback, but is simple not enough. Choosing other business related groups such as LinkedIn can help you connect with other entrepreneurs. LinkedIn is where potential customers and (employees) can find your business. It might not be as popular as face book or twitter, but is proven to be a useful social media tool. It's definitely a great tool for entrepreneurs and business professionals looking to network and establish connections.

✓ Business Card—Creating a business card is an affordable way to make a first lasting impression. If you can design it yourself is a plus, but if you need assistance, there's a lot of companies that can do the job for you are an affordable price. Overnightprints.com is an affordable way to start your business card. Don't forget to match Font and graphics with your business!

✓ Create your web site—A web site is an important tool so potential customers can get to know your business and services. It's important to present your professional information, product and services in a clear manner. Make it simple to navigate. Wix.com let you build a great professional looking website in no time, with their easy to use tools. You can make it as simple or as your unique set of skill level. This website program is what I'm using to build my own website. My husband and I work hard on the creation of my site; he did the harder work of course! Adding some flash elements that make it look great. The full-featured website-building tool is totally free. If you want to remove adds from your site or have your own domain name, the paid subscription runs from $5 to $16 per month, which is pretty affordable!

✓ Write Marketing and a social media marketing plan—It's time to identify marketing tactics. Brainstorm different ideas to reach your target population with your valuable message. Ask friends to help you by generating ideas. Don't censor any idea even if you think is on the wild side. Be creative and pick at least five activities ideas that you can carry out within your budget!

✓ Social media marketing plan can include, promoting your web site, connect with potential customers in LinkedIn, making your Face book image more professional, Using twitter to retweet content that is interesting to your customers, a couple of tweets a day will be good enough! Creating an addictive blog with readers coming back for more!

✓ Network—Develop a plan to find and make connections with key business contacts

✓ Protect your work—copyright, trademarks, and patent—copyright protects original work and ownership, on the other hand patents protect your own invention or a discovery. You might want to consider a trademark if your name is what represent or identify your company or brand

Deliver top quality Customer service—As soon as your customer enters or make a call to your shop it is important to make them feel welcome and that their business with you are well appreciated. Whether is greet by you, a receptionist or sales representative a customer needs to feel a welcoming environment at all times. You want to make sure that everyone that walk through the doors of your shop, don't just do it once but become a returning customer. Growing and maintaining your customers is crucial for your business to grow and move forward. The only way you can achieve this is to demonstrate quality service and products and a superior customer service.

✓ Hire wisely—Your employees should have all the characteristics that will make your business flourish. They should demonstrate excellent customer service. Remember that your employee will be the face of your business so you don't want a worker that misrepresents who you are.

Be a good business role model—As a business owner you have the opportunity to make a positive and memorable impression with your employees and customers. It is important to focus on always delivering a professional image. Focus on encouraging every employee's creativity, quality service and leadership skills. Empower those employ instead of approaching them in a disrespectful way. A successful company is built on a solid foundation and values: integrity, honesty, respect. Those values in which you built your business are a vivid representation of your own character. Your excellent leadership example will be a source of encouragement for your employee and for every customer you come in contact with. Keep it up!

Last Notes

Renew your energy girl!

"Everyone is a house with four rooms, a physical, a mental, an emotional, and a spiritual. Most of us tend to live in one room most of the time but, unless we go into every room every day, even if only to keep it aired, we are not a complete person".

—Rumer Godden

$\mathcal{I}$nner Creative Girl, I emphasize the importance of taking care of your well-being as a whole. In order to be healthy there's four dimensions of health that needs to be balance; the physical, mental/emotional, social and spiritual. These dimensions of health are aspects of life that complement each other to create balance, produce wellbeing and satisfaction. Our health is an interaction between these four dimensions. If one aspect is not functioning properly all other aspects are compromise. A healthy lifestyle includes taking care of all four dimensions! How do we do this? Well let's take a look

Renewing your physical dimension- This an important steps that will involve taking care of your physical body, eating a healthy diet, getting enough sleep, relaxation and getting involved in any kind of physical activity that will keep you active and healthy. It could be a fun form of exercise that you enjoy the most. I personally enjoy antigravity yoga, hip hop yoga, zumba fitness or any dance class. Activities I enjoy the most are rollerblading, beach Volley ball and other fun sports. The good news is that you have a variety of physical activity you can choose from and make your own exercise RX.

Renewing your spiritual dimension—Practicing your beliefs can provide meaning and direction to your life. Our commitment to our value system can help us by giving us a sense of purpose to our lives. People practice various things very useful to them—praying, meditating, reading the Bible, inspirational books, listening to music that elevates them or a nature walk. Do what you enjoy the most and renew your spiritual self daily.

Renewing your mental/emotional—Keep your brain active by Reading, writing, learning new skills and exercising your thinking. A good emotional exercise will be to practice being grateful, pursue a passionate interest like taking an art class, volunteer for a worthy cause or just doing something good for someone else will make you feel good. These types of mental strengths can boost your overall quality of life.

Renewing your social dimension—It's the ability to interact with the people around you. Social support and growth are essentials for living a healthy life and achieving goals. Acquiring social and leadership skills is crucial to sustain and build good lasting relationships within society. It's important to use good communication skills, enhance and create support systems that include family and friends, respect yourself and others.

Balance renewal

It's a great satisfaction to discover where you headed in life. Is something I wish I would new earlier in my life. But I'm one of those inner creative girls that think that the past don't really matter but what you are becoming today. I don't regret my life experiences because otherwise I wouldn't be writing this inspirational book about how I got to discover my true career passion. I see those learning experiences as tools to help others that have gone through a similar experience in their life. Now that we know our passion and the career path we want to undertake, the adventure is not over yet. We need to plan to maintain a happy, balance and fulfilled life as we continue our journey as an entrepreneur girl! I know that every beginning is difficult and we might have to work more than usual to make it happen. But more importantly we need to create a balance. If you're a mom and a wife there's other task that you need to take care of. That's a reason to always plan ahead and maintain a schedule with important activities aside from work. Your family is another important investment in your life and you don't want to be careless about it. Seek help, don't take the role of a super woman, but ask for support from your husband, another family member or a trustful friend when you need it. Taking time for yourself is also important, is a date in your calendar that you can't afford to neglect. Taking even a few minutes away from work will keep you re-energize and will help you being more proactive in your work. Working all of the time will definitely burn you out. You can fit into your schedule a early in the morning relaxation bath before doing anything else or late at night when everything have been done.

GET INSPIRE

Every year develop the habit to create a list of quotes that guide and inspire you throughout the year! Here are my favorites for this year 2013:

"Obstacles are necessary for success because in selling, as in all careers of importance, victory comes only after many struggles and countless defeats."

Og Mandino

"Take care of your body. It's the only place you have to live."

Jim Rohn

"If you are going to achieve excellence in big things, you develop the habit in little matters.

Excellence is not an exception, it is a prevailing attitude."

—*Charles R. Swindoll*

"Leadership is not magnetic personality—that can just as well be a glib tongue. It is not 'making friends and influencing people'—that is flattery. Leadership is lifting a person's vision to high sights, the raising of a person's performance to a higher standard, the building of a personality beyond its normal limitations."

—*Peter F. Drucker*

"Strength does not come from winning. Your struggles develop your strengths. When you go through hardships and decide not to surrender, that is strength."

—*Arnold Schwarzenegger*

"Success is not the key to happiness. Happiness is the key to success. If you love what you are doing, you will be successful."

—*Albert Schweitzer*

"Study while others are sleeping; work while others are loafing; prepare while others are playing; and dream while others are wishing."

—William Arthur Ward

"Yesterday is not ours to recover, but tomorrow is ours to win or lose."

—Lyndon Johnson

"If we did all the things we are capable of, we would astound ourselves."

—Thomas Edison

"My attitude is that if you push me towards something that you think is a weakness, then I will turn that perceived weakness into a strength."

—Michael Jordan

TAKE ONE STEP AT A TIME

You need to take one step at a time if you want to avoid unnecessary stress and frustration. Sometimes I wish everything I'm envisioning can happen in a blink of an eye. In reality things don't work that way. Every time an overwhelming tough come into my mind I start thinking of a little baby. A baby doesn't born with the ability to walk right away, is a process that takes time, effort and a lot of falling in the attempt to walk. We have to concentrate in work step by step in achieving our goals and soon we will see the results of our hard work. Focus on what needs to be done first, set priorities and you'll get there at the right time. Hope these lyrics by Jordan Sparks can motivate you to be a little patience as you start seeing the results of your hard work and dedication.

> Hurry up and wait
> So close, but so far away
> Everything that you've always
> dreamed of
> Close enough for you to taste
> But you just can't touch
>
> One step at a time there's no
> need to rush It's like learning to
> fly or falling in love It's going
> to happen when . . . .

COUNT YOUR BLESSINGS!

A grateful person is always counting their blessings! I make a decision to count my blessing every day, because it motivates me to continue working hard in life. I bought a cute thank you birthday card to remind me every year how thankful I have to be to God for all He has done in my life. I thank God for giving me the opportunity to create, to give back to others with the talents I have been gifted with. I hope you enjoy every detail of your new life adventure as an entrepreneur girl and be grateful to get to this point in your life. Move forward every day and conquer the world around you with a grateful heart. I wish you the best in your journey to achieve your dearest dreams!

About the Author

*C*arol Ramos became a leader since she was nineteen years old. While working as a volunteer at her local church she created a youth magazine and a youth organization. Working at different prevention organizations, navigating college life and other life experiences motivate her to start her own business. She currently lives with her husband in Miami, FL.